Boise State College Western Writers Series   Number 10

Plains Indian Autobiographies

By Lynne Woods O'Brien

Editors: Wayne Chatterton
       James H. Maguire

Business Manager:
       James Hadden

Cover Design by Arny Skov,
Copyright 1973

The Cover Illustration is
Pictograph No. 52 from M. W.
Stirling's "Three Pictographic
Autobiographies of Sitting Bull,"
*Smithsonian Miscellaneous
Collections,* vol. 97, no. 5
(1938), 1-57. Used by per-
mission of the Smithsonian
Institution.

Boise State College, Boise, Idaho

Printed in the United States of America by
The Caxton Printers, Ltd.
Caldwell, Idaho

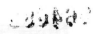

Plains Indian Autobiographies

Plains Indian Autobiographies

The highly nomadic, wealthy, and colorful culture which—with the aid of the horse, the gun, and the buffalo—blossomed on the Great Plains of North America in the early Nineteenth Century constitutes the Plains Indian tribes of this pamphlet: the Blackfoot, Gros Ventre, Plains Cree, Assiniboin, Crow, Sioux, Cheyenne, Shoshoni, Comanche, Kiowa, and Arapaho. (For a concise survey of Plains Indian ethnography, see Harold Driver, *Indians of North America*.)

The word "autobiography" is a European-American term, meaning to write one's own life story or a portion thereof. In order to examine Plains Indian autobiographical forms, I have expanded the definition of autobiography to include oral, dramatic, and artistic expressions by native individuals about their own lives. White autobiography tends to limit itself to "real" or historical events in the autobiographer's present or past life. One form of Plains Indian autobiography, the vision, allows the native autobiographer to explore his future life by spiritual means. Consequently, I have also expanded the term "autobiography" to include future events in the autobiographer's life of which he believes he has supernatural foreknowledge.

Plains Indians traditionally did not tell their entire life stories because the lives of tribal members did not vary enough from one another to warrant a complete recital. Tribes were homogeneous cultural units in which the basic patterns of daily life were the same for all.

Yet autobiographical forms did exist among the Plains Indians. Young children were educated in their family and tribal history by means of stories, many of them autobiographical in origin. Young men strove to distinguish themselves in battle by touching an armed enemy, rescuing a fallen comrade under fire, or stealing a war horse, so that upon their return the older men would invite them to council to tell of their achievements. A man's later civic career as an honored tribal advisor or peace chief depended upon his earlier war record, which he preserved either in oral stories or in pictographic skin paintings.

Religion had as great a part as war in shaping the autobiographical forms of the Plains Indians. Before a young man could go to war, he was supposed to secure the protection of a helper, which might be the spirit of an animal, bird, plant, geographical feature, or mythological being. In order to obtain a protector, the youth went out by himself to fast and pray. If successful, he was rewarded with a vision in which his lifetime helper would promise to protect him in battle. Many times a man's future life or the future fortune of his tribe was predicted in these visions. The vision is a native autobiographical form in that it predetermined the pattern of a man's achievements.

Both the coup story and the vision, which together provided the framework for tribal government and religion, were for the most part the autobiographical province of the Plains Indian man and were preserved in a rich oral and pictographic tradition. The Plains Indian woman had no such cultural forms for making statements about her life. While tanning hides, sewing, or cooking, women undoubtedly talked among themselves and to children about their lives. However, all of these autobiographical expressions were informal. Only a few women's stories told in pre-white times have been preserved by native men while writing their childhood reminiscences. The autobiographies of Plains Indian women which do exist were collected by white anthropologists or frontier historians, specifically to fill the void in European-American knowledge of the Indian woman's life.

When the tribes settled on the reservations, white men came among them as army officers, doctors, missionaries, frontier historians, and anthropologists. As these men came to know the old warriors and medicine men, the whites collected their life histories in order to get the Indian side of frontier battles, to document a religious conversion, or to record a way of life before it was gone forever. These life histories I call the "as-told-to" autobiographies, since that phrase often appears on the title page or in the introduction, indicating that the white man acted as recorder and editor for the Indian informant.

The "as-told-to" autobiographies are as much influenced by the white recorder as by the native author. They could with equal justice be called biographies, since the interests of the recorder often direct the narrative. Because I am interested in how the Plains Indian saw himself, I have chosen to ignore the distinction between biography and autobiography. As long as a book centers on one native informant, I have considered it to be autobiography. Whites often influenced the narrative in these books by asking questions, either about tribal ethnology or about battles that were of particular interest to European-American readers. There are, for instance, three autobiographies which have as their central focus the Custer battle. Certainly, the interest which the Indians have shown in trying to determine who killed Custer has been inspired by the whites, since none of the Indians at the time of the Battle of the Little Big Horn knew or cared that Custer led the troops.

Indian contributions to the form of these "as-told-to" books include examples of traditional native autobiographical forms, especially accounts of the visions which shaped the dreamer's life and repetitious tales of horse raids and war parties—a documentation of the coups which made the raconteur a leader of his people. Rarely in his own culture would a warrior be called upon to narrate all of his coups at once. Yet his white biographer asked him for the story of his life. Thus, every coup had to be told, for coups were the essence of every warrior's life. The repetitious story which results is the unhappy combination of two culturally diverse autobiographical forms.

Many of these "as-told-to" autobiographies end with the beginning of reservation life, even though the Indian may still have been a young man at that time. The sedentary, inglorious, and painful life of the reservation period had no predecessor in Indian experience. No traditional autobiographical form existed in which the new life could find expression. Native thoughts and feelings during that period were too painful to express. For many Indians, what happened in the depressing early reservation years "was not a story."

Some of the very young escaped the worst years of the reservation period, because they were sent off to attend school, usually Captain Pratt's Carlisle Institute in Pennsylvania, the first Indian school in the country. Those students who lived through the violent cultural shock brought about by the forced change in culture and environment learned English as well as a trade before returning to their people. Several of these Eastern-educated Indians later wrote their own autobiographies in English. In these books the authors act as interpreters and apologists for native culture. Standing with one foot in each culture, these authors ultimately came to feel that native moral values were superior to white ones. To varying degrees they rejected white civilization. Although they expressed themselves in books rather than coup stories and visions, they ultimately preferred to define their essential character as Indian.

As the old tribal life slipped away into the distant past, at least one contemporary native autobiographer, N. Scott Momaday, felt the need to recapture its beauty for his own benefit. His autobiography is a statement of love for his native heritage, rather than anger or disillusionment with white culture.

The simplest traditional autobiographical form among the

Plains Indians was the given name. A person's name commemorated some act, quality, or dream either of the person himself or of the relative who named the child originally. The warrior Standing Bear gave all of his children names which kept his honor alive in the minds of family and tribe. Because Standing Bear had killed many enemies in battle, he named his baby son Plenty-Kill. An older boy was named Sorrel Horse because Standing Bear had had a sorrel horse shot out from under him in battle; another boy bore the name Never-Defeated because the father had always been successful in war. A girl was called Feather-Weaver, since Standing Bear owned many beautiful feather ornaments; a second girl was called Two-Staffs, for her father belonged to two warrior lodge societies and each had honored him with a staff (Luther Standing Bear, *My Indian Boyhood,* pp. 155-56).

Children were also named after dream visions or happenings at birth. The grandfather of a Crow baby dreamed that his grandson would count many coups in war; so the child was named Plenty-Coups (Many-Achievements) for his anticipated future actions. This dream, which also foretold that Plenty-Coups would become a chief and would live to be an old man, not only gave the boy the name he bore throughout life, but also motivated him to act like a chief so that he could live up to his name and the expectations of his family (Frank B. Linderman, *Plenty-Coups,* pp. 27-28).

Usually a young man lost his childhood name when he performed some brave action in war. Upon his successful return, he was given a new name which commemorated his deed. Since the Plains Indians considered it rude for a man to brag about himself, the native man traditionally would not tell his name to a stranger. If asked his name, an Indian customarily would turn to a comrade who gave the name, since to speak it himself would be to boast of his achievements.

One of the best ways to earn a good name in Plains Indian

culture was to count coup. *Coup* is a French term, meaning a "blow" or "hit." To prove his courage, a warrior would ride down an armed enemy and touch him with a decorated lance—his coup stick. Degrees of honor—the first, second, third, or fourth coup—were awarded to the first four warriors who struck an enemy. The frontier historian Stanley Vestal describes the process:

> When a man struck his foe, he yelled his own name aloud, adding, "I have overcome this one," so that he might have witnesses to his deed. And as soon as the fight was over, the warriors got together, and each one put in a claim for the honors to which he was entitled. If he could produce witnesses to these, they were formally awarded to him. Thereafter, the winner was entitled to narrate his deed at any public gathering. In fact, he was compelled to do so, for such a war-story formed the invariable credentials of a man performing any public action. (*Sitting Bull,* p. 11)

When a successful war party returned to camp, a victory dance was held to honor it. The warriors sang, danced, and acted out their coups before the assembled village. The women spontaneously composed songs to celebrate the men's deeds. In this context song, dance, and drama were autobiographical forms.

By far the largest number of Plains Indian autobiographical forms were oral—incidental personal adventure and coup stories, names, and songs. Most of these, of course, have been lost. However, the Indian did have a written pictograph language. Pictographs were painted most often upon hides by men who were recording their autobiographies as warriors. At times one or more men might paint the hide, while the "author" stood by telling them what to draw. The hides might serve as clothing (war shirts, leggings, moccasins, or robes), or as the inside lining or outside wall of a tipi.

Horse-stealing and couping were the favorite pictographic subjects, for upon them rested a man's fame. Only rarely was the buffalo painted, in spite of its central importance as the source of food and clothing. Other animals appeared even less frequently.

Because men and horses were painted so often, it is easy to speak of pictographic conventions in relation to them. The figures of both are almost always drawn from the side, although the man's chest may be turned to the front. These figures may be stick-like or fairly detailed. Most of the figures are two-dimensional, outlined in color and then filled in. The action in a pictograph usually moves from right to left, with the autobiographer shown mounted, the enemy either dismounted or in the act of fleeing. Wounds are denoted by a red spray coming from the spot of injury, while heavy fire is often indicated by streaks in the air. Particular hair and clothing styles identify the different tribes of Indians. The passage of time may be shown either by dotted lines representing the path of action or by repeated figures (one fighting, one dead) illustrating simultaneously the action and its denouement. A number of these battle scenes are usually grouped on one robe, sometimes in a spiral arrangement, sometimes along horizontal lines. Only rarely does a single scene cover an entire skin (John C. Ewers, *Plains Indian Painting*, pp. 3-62).

Just as the accomplished warrior had to express his achievements through song, dance, story, or pictograph, the visionary or dreamer had to express his spiritual autobiography through these same forms. Never in Plains Indian culture would a power vision or dream be classified as imaginary. The spiritual world was simply another dimension of the physical world. If a spirit spoke to an Indian in a vision, the Indian guided the rest of his life by its words. According to the Sioux medicine man Black

Elk, "a man who has a vision is not able to use the power of it until after he has performed the vision on earth for the people to see" (John G. Neihardt, *Black Elk Speaks,* p. 208). It may seem strange that the dream of an individual should receive the attention of the entire village, but the medicine man protected the tribe in the spiritual realm much as the warrior protected it in the physical world. And fully as much community attention was due to a man who had had powerful religious experiences as to one who had proved himself a valiant warrior. In Plains Indian society, these were the men whose deeds formed the basis of tribal life. To share his experiences with his tribe each type of man employed the same forms—dance, song, story, and symbol.

When Plains Indians fell under European-American domination, the native's self-concept underwent a change, and consequently so did native autobiographical forms. The native mechanisms for self-realization had been the coup, the coup story, and the vision. But the white man forbade intertribal warfare and frowned upon native religion. In fact, whites tried everything possible to force Indians to "progress" in the white way of doing things. If a man chose to remain a conservative—that is, true to his native traditions—he was tormented by white agents, school teachers, and ministers, as well as by the so-called progressives among his own people. He might, like the Sioux conservatives Sitting Bull and Crazy Horse, even be killed.

Sitting Bull drew a representation of his coups at least three times between 1870 and 1882. In both technique and subject matter, his autobiographies are generally traditional. White influence, shown in such things as his use of paper and pencil, does not interrupt the basic native pictographic design. Even though two of his autobiographies were drawn after his surrender, he never seriously departed from the traditional rules of pictographic composition. Apparently, his image of himself in his society was not destroyed by defeat. He felt no need to explain his actions to whites in white forms. White armies might defeat him, but white culture could not intrude upon the way he saw himself. All three of his autobiographies, the Kimball, Smith, and Pettinger (named after the white men who were instrumental in preserving them), are published in the *Smithsonian Miscellaneous Collections,* vol. 97, no. 5, "Three Pictographic Autobiographies of Sitting Bull," by W. M. Stirling.

The cover illustration of this pamphlet is pictograph number 52 of the earliest, or Kimball, autobiography. It was executed on one of "the loose-leaf roster pages of the Thirty-first United States Infantry" (Stirling, "Three Pictographic Autobiographies . . . ," p. 4). Brown sepia ink was used for the outlines which were filled in with red, blue, and yellow. Army Assistant Surgeon James Kimball explains the action of pictograph number 52: "In a fight with the Crows, Sitting Bull kills and scalps one Indian, and counts 'coup' on another who fired at him barely missing him."

This pictograph illustrates many of the conventions of traditional native autobiography. The autograph or name glyph, here a sitting bull, is attached to the warrior by a line. The horizontal marks of bullets fill the air. The circle which indicates some particular battlework, here a rocky barrier, encloses the action. The medicine of the war shield, an eagle in this case, serves to identify both the warrior and his spirit helper to the initiated. The scalp dangling from the horse's bridle means that that particular horse had been ridden when a scalp was taken. The outstretched bow shows that Sitting Bull is here counting coup rather than attempting to kill his enemy. The Crow, however, is trying to kill Sitting Bull and has just discharged his gun in the Sioux's face. But since no gushing wound is shown, it is clear that he has missed. Sitting Bull wears the horned bonnet which only the very brave could wear, thus indicating that he is no novice warrior. He also wears a trimmed feather in his hair. This may indicate that upon some other occasion, he was the scout who went out first to discover the enemy (L. Standing Bear, *My People the Sioux*, p. 57). Following pictographic tradition, the horse is drawn in outline and filled in with flat color, while the movement of the victor and his horse is from right to left.

The two later autobiographies of 1882 show white influence in more than the drawing materials. In them Sitting Bull substitutes the written English name, "Sitting Bull," for his traditional glyph. However, the written name is placed, like the glyph, in the upper right-hand corner and is attached to the warrior by a similar line. The horses in the later pictographs are realistically rounded and shaded, so much so that people who knew Sitting Bull well could recognize his favorite mounts. In his final autobiography there are three human figures drawn full face instead of in the traditional profile. Possibly these innovations grew out of Sitting Bull's association with the artist Rudolph Cronau, who met him at Fort Buford, where the warrior was detained after his surrender.

Wherever Sitting Bull learned his innovations, they were minor compared with the changes brought about in the pictographic tradition by his nephew, White Bull. In 1931 White Bull drew his coups in color in an old business ledger. However, since he had learned to write Dakota, the Sioux language, he also described the pictured action in words on the same page, making his autobiography a bridge between native and white forms. This unique autobiography, translated and edited by James H. Howard, was published as *The Warrior Who Killed Custer, The Personal Narrative of Chief Joseph White Bull.*

White influence is apparent, however, in new subject matter depicted. Besides the traditional war coups, rescues, and horse raids, White Bull has drawn a tipi in great detail, a typical camp circle, and a self-portrait—subjects never pictured traditionally. The native autobiographer was beginning to feel the need to explain himself and his culture to an alien audience.

White Bull was also influenced by the white people's obsession

14

with the Custer battle. His alleged struggle with Custer is drawn four times instead of the single time which would have been standard. This repetition indicates that the autobiography was composed for whites, especially since another coup on an armed Flathead was considered by Indians as White Bull's bravest deed (Vestal, *Warpath,* pp. 120-21).

Because White Bull wrote the Dakota text himself, stylistic elements which were undoubtedly part of coup storytelling are perceptible in his writing. In telling his coup story, a warrior usually began by identifying himself and his family. White Bull has written his name at the top of each page: "This is White Bull." Following the oral form, he next identified himself with his warrior relatives: "I am the son of Makes-room. I am the nephew of Sitting Bull. One Bull is my brother" (Howard, *Warrior Who Killed Custer,* p. 82). He then described the action of the pictograph. Finally, he brought in the all-important corroboration of witnesses: "This deed was seen by others who will vouch for me and verify that I am telling the truth, my friend" (p. 55). Thus White Bull's Dakota text outlines the basic elements in coup storytelling; it does not, however, give the sense of drama and the excitement of the oral form.

White Bull's pictographic autobiography with accompanying text can be profitably compared to his "as-told-to" autobiography, *Warpath,* written by Stanley Vestal. *Warpath* is divided into three sections. The first, which covers White Bull's youth, is very short, probably because a warrior's youth was not traditionally preserved in any native autobiographical form. Its inclusion here reflects Vestal's attempt to meet the demands of white autobiographical form.

The last section of the book is also very short, dealing with White Bull's life on the reservation. White Bull, like most older Indians, would not speak of reservation life, an existence which he considered ignominious and degrading. In *The Warrior Who*

Killed Custer, he had drawn colorful pictures of his exploits in war, while he had merely listed his later activities on the reservation, giving them no verbal or pictorial elaboration. He could not incorporate his life under white domination into his former image of himself.

The middle section of *Warpath* is very long, detailing White Bull's career as a warrior. Like many other "as-told-to" autobiographies, *Warpath* consists mainly of a long chain of coup stories, for to a warrior the story of his life was synonymous with the story of his coups. Since war plays a major role in European-American histories, frontier authors easily incorporated the native coup story into a white form—the military autobiography. These autobiographies were of interest to whites because they told the Indian side of Western battles. Over and over again descriptions appear of the Fetterman fight, the Wagon-Box fight, Crook's battle on the Rosebud, and Custer's battle on the Little Big Horn. In fact, many of the "as-told-to" autobiographies probably would not have been collected if white and native autobiographical forms had not had such similar concerns in documenting man's bravery in war.

These books are also important because they reveal how the older native man responded to the collision of white and Indian cultures. White Bull, who in his young warrior days had proved himself an incredible daredevil even among the Sioux, later spoke out with the same courage against white corruption. When the Indian Agent tried to get the Sioux to lease their lands to white cattlemen for a very low price, White Bull refused. The agent thereupon locked him in the guardhouse. When the Agent let him out three months later, he told White Bull that he wanted to be his friend. White Bull retorted, "You are a Government Agent, sent here to help the Indians, but instead of doing that you are cheating them. . . . I cannot be friends with a man like that. . . . You are trying to scare me, but you are only scaring yourself. You will be the one afraid of what has been done. . . . This Reservation belongs to the Indians and I will use all my power to make the best of it" (Vestal, *Warpath,* pp. 241-42). The honesty and grand courage which were the life blood of the coup tradition sustained White Bull in his battle with the agent. He had had time to prove himself in the ways which his culture provided, and his sense of self-worth and righteousness gave him the strength to perform, albeit verbally, a fine "coup." As Indians came to deal with whites, criticism of white behavior became an increasingly strong theme in native autobiography.

White Bull was already an established warrior by the time of the Custer Battle in 1876. Thus, both of his autobiographies were shaped by a traditional native autobiographical form—the coup story. Wooden Leg, a Cheyenne, was just eighteen in 1876. And when his people came in to surrender during the winter of 1876-1877, he had few coups to his credit. Consequently, his autobiography, *Wooden Leg, A Warrior Who Fought Custer,* could not be a long chain of coup stories. Instead, its form was shaped by its recorder, Thomas B. Marquis, an agency doctor and amateur historian who had a passion for the Custer battle. Marquis asked Wooden Leg to discuss his youth and his tribe's ethnology in the first half of the book, and to describe the Indians' activities before, during, and after the Custer battle in the second half of the book: "It seemed that his [Wooden Leg's] lifetime biography should surround his special battle story, so that readers might learn what kind of people were the hostile Indians of that day" (p. viii). So the form of *Wooden Leg* points both backward and forward. It is based upon a battle, like an old coup story, yet it includes much ethnographic material solely for the purpose of educating a white audience. As the Indian was forced out of the framework of his own culture, he began to sense white ignorance of Indian culture. In many of the later autobiographies, the Indian author attempts to educate whites as to the true nature of Indian society.

Wooden Leg, like White Bull before him, criticized the white cultural patterns and values which were painfully forced upon him. First, he objected to giving up his gun and his horse. For a man whose honor was won in war and whose occupation was the hunt, surrendering his horse and gun was tantamount to surrendering his manhood. Later, whites forbade reservation Indians to practice their own medicine, and Wooden Leg spoke out for freedom of medicine:

> We had good medicine men in the old times. It may be they did not know as much about sickness as the white men doctors know, but our doctors knew more about Indians and how to talk to them. . . . In present times our Indian doctors are put into jail if they make medicine for our sick people. . . . I think it is best and right if each sick one is allowed to choose which doctor he wants. (Marquis, *Wooden Leg,* p. 365)

Whites also forced monogamy upon the Plains Indians. The constant warfare had meant that there were usually more women than men in a tribe, and a man often married two or three women, usually sisters. As Indian judge, Wooden Leg not only had to divorce one of his own wives, but had to order other men to follow suit. His criticism of white highhandness in setting families asunder asserted itself in passive resistance:

> Afterward, from time to time, somebody would tell me about some man living a part of the time at one place with one wife and a part of the time at another place with another wife. I just listened, said nothing, and did nothing. These were old men, and I considered it enough of a change for them that they be prevented from having two wives at the same place. (p. 369)

The autobiographies of Sitting Bull, White Bull, and Wooden

Leg illustrate how the native coup story was incorporated into the white military autobiography. In addition, these books show how the Native American's resistance to white encroachments did not end with his military defeat. When the native man could no longer fight with weapons, he fought with words and thus maintained his integrity. Later, as white regulations became more stringent, he learned passive resistance and fought with silence.

Another native autobiographical form, the vision, also made its way through the transition period. Whites could not forbid Plains Indians to have visions, but they did make every attempt to end native religion by converting the Indians to Christianity. The vision, however, was the native's primary form for defining his life in relation to the powers of the universe. After the collapse of traditional native religion, the vision re-emerged in the Native American Church.

First, the vision operated to define a man's life within traditional native society. *Two Leggings, The Making of a Crow Warrior,* by Peter Nabokov, illustrates how the lack of a powerful vision could prevent a native man from becoming a tribal leader. Since Two Leggings was first of all a warrior and not a medicine man, his story makes very clear the relation between a man's dream and his success or failure in war. Without a powerful helper obtained through a vision, a man could not become a pipeholder (the leader of a war party), for he would have no means by which to protect his followers. Thus, at the outset he would be prevented from advancing up the ladder of tribal leadership.

Two Leggings was an orphan who wanted above all else to become a chief; yet no matter how often nor how long he fasted, his dreams were never powerful enough to convince the tribal leaders that he had been blessed with a strong spirit helper. These leaders urged him to conquer his ambition and to wait for his power to come. But the young man was too headstrong.

He defied the chiefs and medicine man by continuing to lead war parties, until several hairbreadth escapes convinced him that tribal authority and the spiritual powers could not be flouted. Only then did he submit his ego to the discipline of an elder. From Chief Sees-the-Living-Bull, Two Leggings "bought" a war medicine bundle. He had to follow this Chief's advice and dreams in order to learn where to lead his next war party. Ultimately, Two Leggings actually became a pipeholder, but his failure to have a powerful vision prevented him from realizing his lifetime ambition of becoming a chief.

In psychological terms, the Crow leaders felt that Two Leggings was unbalanced. He was all bravery unmixed with deference to the wisdom of elders. He was too passionate in his own cause to be able to put the cause of the people first. He was willing to risk the lives of his comrades to forward his own reputation. His bravery would make him a fine minor war officer, but his lack of self-control disqualified him as a statesman.

Two Leggings is unique among the "as-told-to" autobiographies because it depicts a native man at war with his own culture. The man was so obsessed with the attempt to achieve recognition within the framework of native society that he felt his life finished when the framework collapsed. The Crows settled on their reservation in 1875 when Two Leggings was only thirty-one, and he lived to be seventy-nine. Yet after he describes his last horse raid, he ignores the rest of his life: "Nothing happened after that. We just lived. There were no more war parties, no capturing of horses from the Piegans and the Sioux, no buffalo to hunt. There is nothing more to tell" (Nabokov, *Two Leggings,* p. 197).

Another Crow, Plenty-Coups had a vision when he was nine years old which not only helped him to become a chief but also set in motion the Crow policy of peaceful relations towards whites. His autobiography, *Plenty-Coups, Chief of the Crows,* as told to Frank Bird Linderman, was written for the express purpose of helping whites to understand Indians better. Although the book contains a description of tribal customs and a series of Plenty-Coups' war stories, his vision provides the basic structure of the book as it did of his life. At the beginning, another old warrior comments, "Your medicine-dream pointed the way of your life, and you have followed it" (p. 5).

Plenty-Coups' vision came to him after he had gone for days without food or water and had sacrificed the end of a finger to the Helpers. In it he follows a "Man Person" through a long tunnel filled with thousands of buffalo. The Man Person calls the buffalo up out of the ground until the Plains are covered with them. But suddenly all the buffalo disappear. Out of the hole in the ground the Man Person calls a new grazing animal —spotted bulls and cows and calves. Next, the Man Person takes Plenty-Coups back through the ground until the two come out exactly where Plenty-Coups' house is later to be built. Here the boy sees his house of the future, and in the shade of the trees he sees himself—a feeble old man.

A sudden change in the vision brings Plenty-Coups to the edge of a beautiful forest. Suddenly a terrible storm strikes the trees, and they "twist like blades of grass and fall in tangled piles," for "the Four Winds that always make war alone had this time struck together. . . ." Only one tree is left standing. In it, his spiritual guide tells him, the chickadee has built its nest. "He is least in strength but strongest of mind among his kind. He is willing to work for wisdom. The Chickadee-person is a good listener. . . . He gains success and avoids failure by learning how others succeeded or failed, and without great trouble to himself. . . . Develop your body, but do not neglect your mind, Plenty-Coups. It is the mind that leads a man to power, not strength of body" (Linderman, *Plenty-Coups,* pp. 59-67).

Upon his return to camp, the council heard and interpreted Plenty-Coups' vision. The boy had been told that he would see the buffalo disappear forever, to be replaced by the white man's

21

cattle, that his life would change its pattern until in his old age he would live in a house like a white man. The storm of the Four Winds was the war which the whites would wage against the Plains tribes. All but one tribe would be destroyed, for the whites were too powerful. That one tribe, the Crow, would keep their homeland, because like the chickadee they would watch the problems of others, and profit from others' mistakes. At the very end of his vision, Plenty-Coups had been told to avoid a lodge that contained baby clothes. The old men of the council told him that this meant that he would have no children.

Plenty-Coups guided his own life and Crow policy towards whites by this vision. Everything came to pass as shown in the vision. Although he married, he had no children who lived. Twenty-six years after his vision, white hunters slaughtered the last of the great buffalo herds. Cattle appeared in their place. Because the Crow never made war on the whites, the tribe was allowed to stay in its ancestral homeland on a reservation of its choosing. Plenty-Coups' house was finally built on the exact spot where he had seen it as a boy of nine.

There is no doubt that the Crow policy of making peace with whites had begun before Plenty-Coups' vision. As a boy he may well have heard older men discussing tactics in regard to whites. The Crow were surrounded by hostile tribes which attacked them regularly. They could not afford to fight whites in addition to their traditional enemies. Most Indian tribes, however, first tried to deal peaceably with whites but were forced by recurring injustices and treaty violations to fight at last. The fact that the Crow never fought the whites is probably due in large part to Plenty-Coups' vision.

Plenty-Coups' policy of keeping peace with whites did not mean that he liked the newcomers. As an older man he was critical of white hypocrisy: the whites insisted that Indians observe laws which the whites broke with impunity; the whites insisted that the Indians follow white religion when whites

22

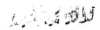

could not agree with one another on the subject (Linderman, *Plenty-Coups,* pp. 227-28). Plenty-Coups, who tried to take several white men along on a winter trip to recover stolen horses, complained that the whites thought only of camping, sleeping, and eating. They wore too many clothes, yet they were always freezing. They ran their horses until the animals could scarcely walk, and when the fight finally began, the men did not know enough to get to cover, and all but one were shot (pp. 228-33).

In Plenty-Coups' opinion, one of the worst results of white domination was that war parties were no longer allowed, and consequently, the Crow no longer developed quick minds and active bodies. Plenty-Coups' vision had instructed him to obtain both. He had seen what happened to whites who had neither, and he feared for the future of his people.

Plenty-Coups' character was not broken during the transition period, because his vision had prepared him with a pattern which organized his life and made his experience understandable. He did not like reservation life, but he was able to endure it. By farming, building a house, and opening a trading store, he led the way in acculturation. He had the foresight and the balanced judgment which Two Leggings lacked. During the early reservation period his people made him a chief.

If Plenty-Coups' vision showed him how to live with the White man, Black Elk's did not. Black Elk told his story to the poet John G. Neihardt in 1931, and the latter published it as *Black Elk Speaks, Being the Life Story of a Holy Man of the Oglala Sioux.* The book is divided into five major periods: Black Elk's early boyhood, the historic battles of Sioux resistance, Black Elk's emergence as a medicine man, his trip to Europe with the Buffalo Bill show, and the Ghost Dance tragedy. But throughout these varied topics runs one theme. In Black Elk's words, it is "the story of a mighty vision given to a man too weak to use it; of a holy tree that should have flourished in a people's heart with flowers and singing birds, and

23

now is withered; and of a people's dream that died in bloody snow" (p. 2).

Black Elk was born in 1863. His father and several of his uncles were medicine men. Crazy Horse, the great Sioux war leader, was his second cousin. When the Sioux wars of resistance began, Black Elk's father chose to remain with the independents, away from the agencies. He called the Sioux chiefs Red Cloud and Spotted Tail "cheap men" because they sold Indian land to whites. Black Elk, traveling with the independents, saw or heard about all of the great battles of the Sioux. At age thirteen he fought Custer's forces at the Little Big Horn. At fifteen he was one of Sitting Bull's small band which fled to Canada. As a child Plenty-Coups knew from the conversation of his elders that whites had to be accommodated. The young Black Elk, on the other hand, heard only scorn for the accommodationists of his tribe. By the time he had his great vision at age nine, he undoubtedly felt that great difficulties were ahead for his people. If the Sioux warriors could not stop the white advance, if destruction were to fall upon his tribe, then only the medicine men would be able to lead the tribe back to physical and spiritual well-being.

Black Elk's Great Vision, which came to him when he was in a coma, is probably the most gorgeous and spectacular Plains Indian dream ever recorded. The vision begins when two spirit messenger men who fly like arrows take him to the sky world, where "his grandfathers" await him. The grandfathers are the spirits of the six directions—west, north, east, south, earth, and heaven—of Sioux cosmology. Black Elk has been summoned by the powers of the world. In the sky world he is first received by a bay horse who calls together a retinue of horses to escort the boy to the great meeting with the grandfathers. These horses come in groups of twelve and are the color of the direction from which they come: twelve blacks with manes of lightning and "thunder in their nostrils" come from the stormy west; twelve white horses with manes "flowing like a blizzard wind" come from the snowy north; twelve sorrels or reds with "eyes that glimmer . . . like the day-break star and manes of morning light" come from the dawning east; twelve buckskins or yellows "with manes that live . . . and [grow] like trees and grasses" come from the summery south. In the horse dance which follows, the sky is filled with flashing, prancing, neighing horses of all colors. At the conclusion of the dance the horses turn into all the beasts and birds of the world and return "to the four corners of the world" (Neihardt, *Black Elk Speaks*, pp. 23-25).

In Sioux cosmology each direction has its own color and symbol, its own psychological and physical characteristics. For example, the west is black with storm and can represent conflict or the chance to overcome physical or spiritual drouth. The north is white with snow and can represent physical health, wisdom, and the endurance that comes from struggle. The east is red, filled with pure morning light, spiritual illumination, and peace. The south is yellow or green, the colors of growth, warmth, innocence, and childhood, the beginnings of life. All life experiences and human traits have their place in the great medicine wheel of the four directions. All are blessed by the sky above them and nourished by the earth below. For the Plains Indian, the medicine wheel was the philosophic framework of the Universe.

After his welcome by the horse dancers, Black Elk proceeds into a cloud tipi with a rainbow door for his meeting with the six grandfathers. Each grandfather meets him in turn and gives him a gift or a prophecy. At the conclusion of this meeting, Black Elk has many powers. In addition, the grandfather of the South has told him that he will lead his people through "four ascents" or generations, traveling both the easy and the difficult roads of life.

Up to this point in the vision, Black Elk has been the passive recipient of the various gifts. Now that he has everything needful to preserve his people—the powers of life, destruction, growth, curing, peace, and rejuvenation—he begins to take an active role in his vision. All of the horses turn into his people, whom he leads down the easy and the difficult roads of life. On this symbolic journey, he has the chance to use his newly acquired gifts. By means of them, he saves his tribe from drouth, disease, famine, and war. For a while, all is fine. His tribe begins the four ascents, or generations, foretold earlier. The first ascent is green and easy. Everyone is happy. The second is steeper, and the people change into all the animals of the world, and all are filled with fear. The third ascent is terrible. Each creature goes his own way, following his own small vision. The nation's hoop, or unity, is broken. The fourth ascent looks the worst of all. However, Black Elk sees that somehow his people will live through it. He sees that the people's sustenance, the buffalo, will disappear, but in its place will come "another strength," a strange herb which blooms in four colors. With the power of the four-colored herb, Black Elk will be able to rejuvenate a sick world. He will be able to turn the pestilential fourth descent into a green and dancing day.

Having demonstrated his ability to save his people, Black Elk is taken to the highest mountain in the Black Hills, Harney Peak. Here he gains an overview of life which gives him understanding of how all life forms must co-exist in harmony: "I saw that the sacred hoop of my people was one of many hoops that made one circle . . ." (Neihardt, *Black Elk Speaks,* p. 43). This understanding becomes the cornerstone of Black Elk's philosophy, his answer to the threatened destruction of his people. The Sioux will survive, for like all other life forms, they have their place in the great wheel of the Universe.

At last Black Elk is taken back to the sacred tipi where the six grandfathers welcome his triumphant return and give again their sacred gifts. Soon after, he finds himself regaining consciousness at home.

In form, Black Elk's vision has seven major sections: the initial call, the horse welcome, the initial gift-giving by the six grandfathers, Black Elk's trial leadership of his people through the four ascents, Black Elk's trip to Harney Peak where he comes to understand the unity of all things, his triumphant return to the six grandfathers, who reaffirm their gifts, and his trip back to his parents' tipi. Many Plains Indian visions contain such things as power gifts, spirit people or animals, forecasts of future events, and autobiographical predictions. Black Elk's vision is unique in that it contains them all. For a nine-year-old boy, he had an incredible understanding of the whole of Sioux cosmology.

If the boy's elders were worried about the tribal future, and possibly even the tribe's continuing existence, as seems more than likely, the sensitive young Black Elk, born into a family of medicine men, had every inducement to dream a powerful vision. By marshalling all the forces of Plains Indian religion against the unknown terror of the white man, Black Elk was able to envision a future for his people on the other side of the debacle, the terrible fourth ascent. On that day all creatures would be relatives, all peoples would live in harmony, all nations would form the "many hoops that made one circle" (Neihardt, *Black Elk Speaks,* p. 43) .

Black Elk kept his vision a secret until he was seventeen because he felt his people would not believe a young boy could have such a powerful vision. Finally his fear of abusing his power by ignoring it drove him to tell a medicine man about his dream. With the help of the village, the dream was performed, and afterwards Black Elk became an acknowledged medicine man, using his grandfathers' gifts to heal the sick. Although he was able to cure people, he was still unhappy, because it was the Sioux nation itself he wished to help. "If a man or woman or child dies, it does not matter long, for the nation lives on. It was the nation that was dying, and the vision was for the nation . . ." (Neihardt, *Black Elk Speaks,* p. 184) .

By this time the Sioux were already settled on reservations. In order to discover how to use his vision to help his people, Black Elk decided to join the Buffalo Bill Show so that he could understand the white world better. However, among the whites, he felt like a man who had never had a vision. All he learned from his travels was "that the Wasichus [whites] did not care for each other the way our people did before the nation's hoop was broken" (Neihardt, *Black Elk Speaks,* p. 221).

Discouraged, he returned to the Pine Ridge Reservation shortly before the Ghost Dance religion swept his people in 1890. The basic tenet of this religion was that a new world was coming to wipe out the present one. Only those who performed the required rituals in dance and song would live. The new world would be the same as the old Indian world before the whites destroyed it. There would be plenty of Buffalo; all one's dead relatives would once more be alive; and there would be no whites. At first, Black Elk was skeptical of the new religion; however, when he saw one of the dances he was amazed at how much of it reminded him of his own vision. Because of this similarity, he decided to help the Ghost Dancers with his power.

The white agent at the Pine Ridge Reservation was afraid that the Ghost Dancers were planning an uprising and called in the troops. In actuality, the Indian people, although starving and desperate, were without sufficient arms to fight, and they planned to rid themselves of whites only by religious means. What Black Elk and the other dancers might have been able to accomplish will remain a mystery, for when the troops massacred Big Foot's band at Wounded Knee, the Ghost Dance religion came to an end. The "people's dream . . . died in bloody snow." Although Black Elk escaped the massacre, his spirit was broken and bitter. His people seemed doomed to poverty, starvation, and disease. His vision, noble as it was, could not help them.

In despair, Black Elk retired to his small, grey, square house to ponder where he went astray. To the end he blamed himself for not following his first great vision, for getting sidetracked by the Ghost Dance and by other smaller visions. "It is hard to follow one great vision in this world of darkness and of many changing shadows. Among those shadows men get lost" (Neihardt, *Black Elk Speaks,* p. 254).

Among the Plains Indian men who have left their life histories behind them, Black Elk stands out as a tragic hero of classic proportions. His belief in the ways of his people was so powerful that he could not, like Plenty-Coups and the Crows, make the painful but necessary accommodation to white greed and lies. He was a cultural pluralist, believing that the "many hoops" of all the nations make one "great circle"; he was a religious environmentalist, believing that men and animals, rivers and stars are all relatives. Unhappily, his conquerors believed that European-American culture was the only true culture and that the universe with all its riches was created to serve that culture. In such a philosophic framework, Black Elk's vision was doomed.

When Plains Indians began to convert to Christianity, they did not stop having visionary experiences, but the symbolic system used to interpret visions changed. A Baptist missionary, F. L. King, was responsible for the conversion of Left-Hand, one of the oldest and most respected Arapaho chiefs. According to his own account, Left-Hand was forty years old before he ever saw a white man. Twenty-nine years later he was a Baptist who repudiated his early life as a warrior: "As I grew older all of my time was taken up on the war path. Finally, I got to scalping and murdering just as the other Indians did. . . . I was thought of as a brave man because I killed men" (King, *Chief Left-Hand,* p. 3). When he became a Baptist, Left-Hand gave up the native cultural framework which made his actions honorable. His new Christian point of view reduced the native system of military honor to undifferentiated "scalping and murdering."

Left-Hand converted because he had two visions. In the first he was not allowed in the church because he was not a Christian. He very much wanted to be inside because the "minister . . . was going to search for the root of all sickness and put it away, so that the end of the world would come sooner" (King, *Chief Left-Hand,* p. 9). Left-Hand began encouraging the Arapaho to attend church and convert. In his second vision, "Heaven seemed to be opened, and I saw and could read in it a black streak [his former life], but did not want to look at that, but looked at the book [Bible]" (p. 9). After this vision, Left-Hand became a Baptist. Compared to the complex symbolism of traditional Plains Indian visions, these visions are starkly simple. The rich religious and philosophic thought of men like Plenty-Coups and Black Elk is reduced to "a black streak," Left-Hand's former life, while the new religious system is understood only as "a book." Yet for Left-Hand, as for Plenty-Coups and Black Elk, the pattern of his future life is still set by vision.

In the area of religion, much of the conflict between native and white forms of worship was resolved by the spread of the peyote religion or Native American Church. Many interesting facts on the peyote religion can be found in "The Autobiography of a Kiowa Indian" by Weston LaBarre. The new church combined aspects of both white and native religion. Similar to white churches, it accepted the Holy Trinity and Christian ethics. More like traditional Indian worship, it had at its heart the individual vision in which the visionary obtained spiritual power from a guide or helper. Often the Indian would make the call of his animal helper during his vision. Like the former medicine men, peyote priests could effect cures by singing over patients and sucking the disease-causing foreign objects out of their bodies.

In the transition from Native-American to white ways, the Indian for the most part lost contact with his language and customs. By preserving the personal vision of the individual, the

Native American Church allowed the Indian to convert to Christianity without losing the mechanism by which he had always placed his own life in its universal context. The autobiographical or life-directing function of vision continued.

The Plains Indian woman traditionally did not seek visions nor fight in war. Nor did she tell of her life in any formalized autobiographical patterns. She did not even have to earn her own name. Perhaps because there was no native tradition of women's autobiography, perhaps because the collectors were nearly always men, perhaps because whites were interested principally in tales of war or vision, only a very few women's autobiographies have been collected. Of these, only one is of major importance: *Pretty-Shield, Medicine Woman of the Crows,* by Frank Bird Linderman.

Linderman maintains his presence as audience and questioner throughout the narrative. In fact, it is his questions which shape and direct Pretty-Shield's story. Since she has neither a central vision nor a collection of war stories to give her narrative cohesion, she sometimes falters in her storytelling. At such times, Linderman asks her general questions about Crow customs or legends to get her started again. The resultant autobiography with its mixture of personal story, history, and legend is true to the spirit of a Plains Indian woman's life. While Linderman is no child, his prodding operates to bring forth story after story just as an Indian child's questions would have done.

In Plains Indian society the grandmother's principal occupation was the care and education of young children. Stories such as Pretty-Shield's formed the backbone of an Indian child's early education. And Linderman often remarks how fond Pretty-Shield is of her grandchildren, how she regularly interrupts her narrative to minister to their needs.

As a grandmother, Pretty-Shield fills her role in traditional Indian society generally with contentment. She laments the fact that the young are beginning to follow immoral white ways, drinking and disobeying their elders. However, in general she expresses joy and happiness in remembering her life as a Crow woman. The few places where she criticizes her society in its treatment of women are fascinating.

Principally, her criticism centers on the failure of native men to recognize and honor women's achievements in war and medicine-making. As a girl, she and her playmates had once killed a buffalo calf and had another time robbed the body of a dead Sioux warrior. Still another time when the Crow camp was being attacked, she had set up her playhouse tipi so as to close a gap in the camp circle and thereby to keep the enemies out of the inner village. Courageous herself, she liked bravery in men or women and felt it should be honored wherever it appeared.

Crow men, however, never mentioned the bravery of women in war, either when telling coup stories among themselves or when talking to whites. Pretty-Shield always asks Linderman whether he has already heard the particular story about a woman's bravery which she is preparing to tell. Never can he say "yes." As a child, Pretty-Shield had watched a sixty-year-old Crow woman drive the attacking Sioux away by riding at them armed only with her root digger and singing her medicine song. Yet the men do not like to hear about that battle because it was won by a woman. When General Crook fought Crazy Horse on the Rosebud, two Crow women went with the warriors to help the soldiers. One "woman" was actually a transvestite; the other, wild and brave, went to war to avenge the death of her brother, recently killed by the Sioux. Working together, they managed to rescue a wounded Crow, count coup, shoot and scalp an armed enemy, all among the most honorable actions of war. Yet, as Pretty-Shield remarks bitterly, the men do not speak of these achievements. Women's history in war is ignored.

Medicine women were as rare as women warriors and not offered much more encouragement. (In spite of the sub-title, *Medicine Woman of the Crows*, little information is given regarding Pretty-Shield's doctoring, although she did have a vision in which the ants became her helpers.) Pretty-Shield told Linderman of her disappointment as a young girl when one of the few Crow medicine women failed to cure a wounded warrior. A noted medicine man had already tried unsuccessfully to cure the man before the medicine woman was called. For Pretty-Shield, then, the cure was terribly important. She so badly wanted the woman to succeed that when the man died she felt drained, exhausted, and old. Clearly, at this point she became depressed because she identified herself with the hoped-for success of the medicine woman. As a girl Pretty-Shield had obviously been critical of the traditionally restricted roles allowed Indian women.

If from time to time Pretty-Shield had felt restricted by her role in Indian society, she was far more bitter about and critical of white greed and corruption. After receiving a fine reservation, the Crows had been reduced to poverty by the white ranchers who leased their lands. So greedy were these men that they shot the Indians' stock so that their own cattle might have every blade of grass. Like so many other older Indians, Pretty-Shield would not talk much about the early reservation period, because her memories of it were all too depressing. The joy and glory of her life lay in the old, free days when the Crow roamed after the buffalo.

With the exception of LaBarre's "Autobiography of a Kiowa Indian," none of these autobiographies deals with white-educated Indians. But some Indians learned English by attending European-American schools. Their autobiographies, which they wrote themselves, begin with the traditional native childhood, follow the author's path through "civilization," and end with a comparison of native and white values. During the years they spent in white schools, many white-educated Indians had to answer questions about native life over and over again. By the time these men decided to write their autobiographies, they knew that the greater part of the job would be to initiate their readers into the customs and ethics of Plains Indian society so that whites would cease seeing Indians as "savages" and would begin realizing their true moral character. Since the Plains Indian had always put the welfare of his tribe ahead of his own material well-being, the role of acting as apologist for his people suited his communal spirit very well. In his apologia he was protecting his people on an ideological and philosophical battlefield, as his ancestors had protected them on the physical and spiritual fronts.

Traditional native autobiographical forms—coup stories, visions, earned names—were embedded in the larger white autobiographical form as childhood memories. Increasingly, however, the native author saw his honesty and his truthfulness, his concern for others and his generosity, as the qualities which made him distinctively Indian. He saw the lack of these qualities as being characteristic of the white man. After having tried hard to explain himself and his people to whites, the native author succeeded in explaining whites to himself. The next step was to show whites how they looked to the Native American. The resultant moral critique of white values touched upon European-American warfare, government, religion, business, education, diet, and health. Two Sioux writers, Charles Alexander Eastman and Luther Standing Bear, provide the best examples of the concerns of the white-educated autobiographer.

Charles Eastman recorded his autobiography in two volumes, *Indian Boyhood* and *From the Deep Woods to Civilization.* The initial volume is expressly a children's book, covering the first fifteen years of his life. Typically, the book opens with the author's earliest recollections and proceeds with a description of an Indian child's education, sports, games, and family life. Many of the adventure tales and tribal legends which Eastman heard as a boy are included. Only in the last chapter is white civilization mentioned. Its cruelties, such as slavery, and its wonders, such as trains, houses, and clocks, are discussed by the boy's elders. But he has no clear conception of white society. Then, suddenly, his father (long thought executed by the whites for his part in the Minnesota Massacre of 1862) returns to the tribe to claim his son. Instead of being hanged, the father has been in prison where he has learned English and converted to Christianity. More important, he has seen that whites would soon outnumber Indians and has come to believe that only by learning the invaders' ways could Native Americans survive. He has returned to the tribe to get his youngest son and to put him in the white man's school. The cultural shock to the fifteen-year-old boy was very great. Eastman says, "I felt as if I were dead and traveling to the Spirit Land; for now all my old ideas were to give place to new ones, and my life was to be entirely different from that of the past" (*Indian Boyhood,* p. 246).

If *Indian Boyhood* documents the sunlit happiness of Eastman's childhood, *From the Deep Woods to Civilization* traces his painful struggle to become an educated Christian man and his terrible disappointment in discovering that white civilization did not live up to its own ideals. His lifetime foray into white culture convinced him at last that native society, though simpler, was of finer moral quality.

Eastman began his schooling in Flandreau, South Dakota, where his father's farm was located. It was Eastman's Indian heritage—to be brave, to obey his father—which sustained him through his traumatic first school days. A year later in 1874 when Eastman left home to go away to school, his father said to him, "Remember, my boy, it is the same as if I sent you on your first warpath. I shall expect you to conquer" (Eastman, *From the Deep Woods . . .* , pp. 31-32).

Once at the missionary boarding school in Santee, South Dakota, Eastman had to struggle with several conflicting cultural values: whites wanted to count and measure everything—turnips, money, and time—while the Indian valued nothing but honor, which could not be bought. Whites valued spelling and reading; the Indian, speech. Whites said that the earth spun around the sun; Indian philosophy and religion said the sun rose in the east and set in the west. However, Eastman dealt with these cultural conflicts as best he could, learned to read, and went to the East for further education while Sitting Bull was still fighting the U.S. Army.

At Dartmouth Eastman enjoyed long philosophic discussions on the comparative merits of Native and European-American cultural values—discussions which arose because of his presence at the College. The East with its refined culture, morality, and art represented to him true Christian civilization, and he felt at home with its values. He completed his formal education in 1890 at the age of thirty-two, graduating from Boston University as a medical doctor. He had followed the white trail to the end, not merely adopting white ways and relinquishing native ones, but resolving apparent cultural conflicts by allowing each culture inherent dignity and integrity.

Eastman's lofty conception of white civilization was challenged when he became the Pine Ridge Reservation doctor in 1890 and witnessed the massacre at Wounded Knee. He was further angered soon after, when agents withheld for themselves ten thousand dollars in payments due to the Sioux, and especially when United States government investigators whitewashed the incident.

Because relations with the agent had become unbearable, Eastman quit his position as agency doctor and moved to Saint Paul, Minnesota, where he opened private practice. Much to his dismay, the citizenry expected him to perform illegal operations or at least to practice "Indian" medicine. In spite of this new disillusionment, he decided to live by the true ideals of Christianity —even though he felt that few whites did—because he believed that Christian principles were in accord with his earlier Indian training.

Some years later Eastman became a lobbyist for Indian treaty rights in Washington, D.C. His greatest shock at white corruption was the discovery that legislators' votes had to be bought (Eastman, *From the Deep Woods . . .* , p. 157). Common justice apparently could not be found even in Washington, D.C.

In spite of his lofty Christian ideals, Eastman came to believe that American civilization was far more brutalized than Plains Indian culture had ever been:

> I am an Indian; and while I have learned much from civilization for which I am grateful, I have never lost my Indian sense of right and justice. I am for development and progress along social and spiritual lines, rather than those of commerce, nationalism, and material efficiency. Nevertheless, so long as I live, I am an American. (*From the Deep Woods . . .* , pp. 194-95)

Luther Standing Bear felt the same, but he was even more outspoken than Eastman. Standing Bear's autobiography spans three volumes, *My Indian Boyhood, My People the Sioux,* and *Land of the Spotted Eagle.* The first is a Sioux ethnology for children, showing especially how Indian children lived. The book is gently but thoroughly propagandistic. In the life of an Indian child, the reader learns, there were many sports and games, much bravery and generosity, little sickness, no dentists, and few dishes. Standing Bear neglects to mention horse stealing, instead suggesting that Indians obtained their animals from wild horse herds. Coup counting is never discussed; in fact, only defensive warfare is mentioned. Clearly, the author was attempting to create good will towards the Indian in the hearts of white children.

Standing Bear's second volume, *My People the Sioux,* is more candid and more personal than his first. Part of his purpose was to present the Sioux to whites "in a true and authentic manner"

(Preface). Just as important were his desire to present his own life and his criticism of white management of Indian affairs. Using his own life as the specific example of the general pattern, Standing Bear presents Sioux life in the early reservation period, at Carlisle Indian School, and in white society. The book is a request for whites to recognize the Native American's intelligence, to grant him citizenship, and to allow him to take his rightful place in building the country's future.

For reasons similar to Eastman's, Standing Bear decided to go to the East to school when he was just ten years old. The Sioux had fought their last battle before Standing Bear was old enough to prove his bravery in war. Yet his father had often said to him that he would rather have his son die honorably on the battlefield than live to be old and weak. When the Carlisle recruiters came, Standing Bear at once volunteered, not to get a white education, for he did not really understand what that meant, but rather to prove to his people that he dared to go unarmed amidst the enemy. He planned to do some brave deed, to escape if he could, and to return to his people. Both Eastman and Standing Bear went to the East so that their fathers would be proud of them. Eastman went with some small idea of what a white education meant, while Standing Bear was motivated only by forces within his own culture.

Soon after arriving at Carlisle, the Indian students were asked to pick new white names for themselves from a list written on a blackboard. Standing Bear writes, "When my turn came, I took the pointer and acted as if I were about to touch an enemy" (*My People the Sioux,* p. 137). The Plains Indian earned his own name by performing some brave act, and Standing Bear was trying to prove his bravery by attending Carlisle. The boy's counting coup on the blackboard symbolized his attempt to explain his new experience in the traditional framework of his culture. But the courage needed to face the long and lonely days of living away from home was different from the spectacular daring which Standing Bear had expected to have to demonstrate. Nevertheless, he endured the shame of having his hair cut, his language banned, his native clothing confiscated, and his familiar diet changed. In the too-rapid transfer to white ways, many native children died. Standing Bear, however, distinguished himself; and to exemplify Carlisle's progress in civilizing the Indian he was chosen to work for the huge Philadelphia department store of John Wanamaker. Standing Bear adjusted well and rose rapidly in Wanamaker's employ. He quit his job only when he tired of searching unsuccessfully for an unprejudiced landlord in Philadelphia.

When he returned to the reservation, Standing Bear found affairs no better. The agent ruled with an iron hand, forcing his will upon everyone, punishing the educated Indians who contradicted him. Only after a long struggle was Standing Bear granted American citizenship and allowed to sell his lands and move off the reservation, away from the control of the agent. Because of his own difficulties in winning American citizenship, Standing Bear objected angrily when the Sioux were drafted to fight in World War I without ever having been made United States citizens. He felt that American prejudice against the Indian made it impossible for the native man to make his proper contribution to the country.

The white prejudice which Standing Bear first identified in *My People the Sioux* was further analyzed in his indictment of white egotism and supremacy in his third autobiographical volume, *Land of the Spotted Eagle:*

> White men seem to have difficulty in realizing that people who live differently from themselves still might be traveling the upward and progressive road of life.
>
> The Lakotas [Sioux] are now a sad, silent, and unprogressive people suffering the fate of all oppressed. . . . Did a kind, wise, helpful, and benevolent conqueror

bring this situation about? Can a real, true, genuinely superior social order work such havoc? Did not the native American possess human qualities of worth had the Caucasian but been able to discern and accept them; and did not an overweening sense of superiority bring about this blindness? (pp. vii-viii)

A good deal of penetrating, thoughtful criticism and hot anger shaped the style of *Land of the Spotted Eagle*. The native who lived for centuries at home in his natural surroundings discovered after his defeat that the white man not only intended to steal his homeland but that he also intended to destroy it by cutting down the forests and slaughtering the animals:

We [Indians] did not think of the great open plains, the beautiful rolling hills, and winding streams with tangled growth as "wild." Only to the white man was nature a "wilderness" and only to him was the land "infested" with "wild" animals and "savage" people. To us it was tame. Earth was bountiful and we were surrounded with the blessings of the Great Mystery. Not until the hairy man from the east came and with brutal frenzy heaped injustices upon us and the families we loved was it "wild" for us. When the very animals of the forest began fleeing from his approach, then it was that for us the "Wild West" began. (p. 38)

Standing Bear saw the white men as unable to accept the new environment into which they had come, and unable to deal justly with the native peoples whom they had robbed. To salve his conscience, the European American claimed to have been "guided by the will of his God; and in so saying absolved himself of all responsibility for his appearance in a land occupied by other men" (*Land of the Spotted Eagle,* p. 249). Because he could write, the white man saw himself as superior to the man who could not; so he called him a "savage." Having thus proved the Indian's "savage" character, the white man set out savagely to destroy him. Standing Bear called for a reversal of this destruction. He believed that "America [could] be revived, rejuvenated, by recognizing a native school of thought" (*Land of the Spotted Eagle,* p. 255).

Luther Standing Bear spoke out strongly for that native school of thought, affirming its "sense of justice, . . . reverence for the rights of life, . . . love for truth, honesty, and generosity, . . . and faith in Wakan Tanka—God of the Lakotas" (*Land of the Spotted Eagle,* p. 258). The glittering brilliance of civilization added nothing, he felt, to the moral qualities of Native-American life.

N. Scott Momaday, the last autobiographer to be considered here, teaches English at the University of California at Berkeley. He is a highly educated and sophisticated man, and his autobiography, *The Way to Rainy Mountain,* is "preeminently the history of an idea, man's idea of himself" (Momaday, *Way to Rainy Mountain,* p. 4). Momaday is not interested in presenting the exterior facts of life, such as when he was born, where he went to school, or what he studied. Instead, he wants the reader to experience the feeling of being Kiowa subjectively, from the inside of the culture. To accomplish this end, he alternates tribal legend, history, and personal memories in a tripartite form. By combining tribal and personal experience, he delineates both his people's discovery of their identity in the journey from mountain tribe to Plains horsemen and his own discovery, retracing that tribal journey, of his Kiowa heritage. When he was a child, Momaday's grandmother had told him the legends of the Kiowa's migration from the Montana Rockies to Rainy Mountain in Oklahoma. After her death, he decided to follow the tribal route himself so that he could live through the great journey in his own mind.

In order to be a whole personality, each Kiowa, Momaday suggests, has to embrace his native heritage and to integrate it into his concept of himself. *The Way to Rainy Mountain* is Momaday's personal response to his Kiowa heritage; it is "the revelation of one way in which these traditions are conceived, developed, and interfused in the human mind" (*Way to Rainy Mountain*, p. 4).

Momaday refuses to make European-American distinctions between autobiography and history, between personal and tribal experience. The journey of self-definition "is a whole journey, intricate with motion and meaning; and it is made with the whole memory, that experience of the mind which is legendary as well as historical, personal as well as cultural" (*Way to Rainy Mountain*, p. 4). The book, then, is a definition of one Kiowa man of himself, within the context of his native heritage.

Although the content of Momaday's autobiography comes from Kiowa culture, the philosophic framework of the book is European-American. "The history of an idea, man's idea of himself" is a modern European-American concept, and a highly intellectual one at that. Traditionally the native man did not differentiate himself from others by the way in which his psyche patterned tribal lore and personal experience into a unique whole. Such a concept of the individual in his culture has its roots in modern psychology and anthropology.

The tripartite form of the book psychologically organizes legendary, historical, and personal experience around the workings of the author's mind and spirit. Each of the twenty-four sections of the book is divided into three sub-sections, each sub-section being printed in a different typeface. The change from one typeface to another indicates a change in time, place, subject, or kind of thought. Using a refined stream-of-consciousness technique, Momaday leads his reader through the processes of his own thought as his mind ranges over legendary mysteries, historical or anthropological fact, and personal memories.

The reader learns not what the Kiowa Momaday did, but rather how he thinks and feels. The author's concern with the culture-making process of the human mind makes *The Way to Rainy Mountain* a book imbued with contemporary European-American thought. The subject matter, however, is Kiowa. And the combination of the two allows the white reader to sense what it must be like to have a Native-American heritage today.

By the time *The Way to Rainy Mountain* was published in 1969, only the oldest native people remembered the pre-white times. With their death, the chain of tribal memory would be broken to a great extent. Consequently, Momaday's concern was to define his Kiowa heritage for himself, rather than for whites. As a result, the tone of his prose is personal, nostalgic, and poetic; it attempts to capture something beautiful before it is gone forever. Momaday has no time to castigate whites for destroying the old life, for such events are "the mean and ordinary agonies of human history" (*Way to Rainy Mountain*, p. 3). In his cultural autobiography he is searching for the sublimity of the past: "a landscape that is incomparable, a time that is gone forever, and the human spirit, which endures" (*Way to Rainy Mountain*, p. 4).

Autobiography, whether oral or written, is the act of expressing oneself about one's own life. What the autobiographer has to say and the form in which he says it are to a large extent predetermined by the culture in which he lives, for his culture gives him the social and historical framework in which he must try to evaluate his life.

The study of Plains Indian autobiography is particularly interesting because it gives a picture of a people in cultural transition. Native culture had autobiographical forms which allowed the Native American to evaluate his life in comparison to those of his fellows and to place it in its universal context. When white people forced an end to Plains Indian warfare and religion, they destroyed the activities by which the Indian had defined himself; consequently they destroyed or seriously altered the forms through which he had expressed that definition. Out of the resultant cultural chaos, the Plains Indian emerged with a new self-definition, one based upon a comparison of white and Indian value systems. Because white people were dominant, the native autobiographer addressed himself principally to them, using their form—the written autobiography. Yet within the white form, he tried to define what it was about himself and his people that remained uniquely Native American.

$Selected$ $Bibliography$

PRIMARY SOURCES

The following list is by no means exhaustive, because Plains Indian auto-biographies are scattered throughout the periodical literature of anthropology, psychology, history, and folklore. Moreover, many of these accounts have titles which in no way indicate their autobiographical nature. Their contents can be determined, consequently, only by examination of each likely work. Many unpublished autobiographies collected by graduate students or amateur historians undoubtedly rest in libraries around the country, waiting for some enterprising researcher to discover them. I believe, however, that the list below contains most of the important published Plains Indian autobiographies.

Pictographic autobiographies painted on skins may be found in museum collections in many cities. I have made no attempt to list these works.

Alexander, Hartley Burr. *Sioux Indian Painting.* Nice, France: C. Szwed-zicki, 1938.

Bass, Althea. *The Arapaho Way, A Memoir of an Indian Boyhood.* New York: Clarkson N. Potter, 1966.

Bent, George. "Forty Years with the Cheyennes." *The Frontier: A Magazine of the West,* vol. 4, nos. 4-9 (Oct. 1905-March 1906) .

Bonnerjea, Biren. "Reminiscences of a Cheyenne Indian." *Journal de la Societe des Americanistes de Paris,* 27 (1935) , 129-43.

Cohoe, William. *A Cheyenne Sketchbook.* Norman: University of Oklahoma Press, 1964.

Courchene, Richard. *Hell, Love and Fun.* Billings, Montana: Richard Courchene, 1969.

Devereux, George. *Reality and Dream, Psychotherapy of a Plains Indian.* New York: International Universities Press, 1951.

Dixon, Joseph K. *The Vanishing Race, The Last Great Indian Council.* New York: Popular Library, 1913.

45

Eastman, Charles A. *From the Deep Woods to Civilization, Chapters in the Autobiography of an Indian.* Boston: Little, Brown, 1931.

———. *Indian Boyhood.* New York: Dover Publications, 1971.

Griffis, Joseph K. *Tahan, Out of Savagery into Civilization.* New York: George H. Doran, 1915.

Grinnell, George Bird. *When Buffalo Ran.* New Haven: Yale University Press, 1920.

Howard, James H. *The Warrior Who Killed Custer, The Personal Narrative of Chief Joseph White Bull.* Lincoln: University of Nebraska Press, 1968.

Hyde, George E. *Life of George Bent, Written from his Letters.* Ed. Savoie Lottinville. Norman: University of Oklahoma Press, 1968.

King, F. L. *Chief Left-Hand, His Life Story.* New York: American Baptist Home Mission Society, n. d.

Kroeber, A. L. "War Experiences of Individuals." *Ethnology of the Gros Ventre.* Anthropological Papers of the American Museum of Natural History, vol. 1, no. 4 (1908), 196-222.

LaBarre, Weston. "The Autobiography of a Kiowa Indian." *Primary Records in Culture and Personality.* Ed. Bert Kaplan. Microcard Publications of Primary Records, vol. 2, no. 14. Madison: The Microcard Foundation, 1957.

Linderman, Frank B. *Plenty-Coups, Chief of the Crows.* Lincoln: University of Nebraska Press, 1962.

———. *Pretty-Shield, Medicine Woman of the Crows.* New York: John Day, 1972.

Long Lance, Chief Buffalo Child. *Long Lance.* New York: Cosmopolitan Book Corporation, 1928.

———. *Redman Echoes, Comprising the Writings of Chief Buffalo Child Long Lance and Biographical Sketches by His Friends.* Los Angeles: Frank Wiggins Trade School, 1933.

Mallery, Garrick. *Picture-Writing of the American Indians.* American Ethnology Bureau Annual Report, 10 (1888-1889).

Marquis, Thomas B. *She Watched Custer's Last Battle.* Hardin: Custer Battle Museum, 1933.

———. *Wooden Leg, A Warrior Who Fought Custer.* Lincoln: University of Nebraska Press, 1967.

McCreight, M. I. *Chief Flying Hawk's Tales, The True Story of Custer's Last Fight.* New York: Alliance Press, 1936.

46

————. *Firewater and Forked Tongues, A Sioux Chief Interprets U.S. History.* Pasadena: Trail's End Publishing Co., 1947.

Michelson, Truman. "Narrative of an Arapaho Woman." *American Indian Anthropologist,* 35 (1933), 595-610.

————. "Narrative of a Southern Cheyenne Woman." *Smithsonian Miscellaneous Collections,* vol. 87, no. 5 (1932), 1-13.

Momaday, N. Scott. *The Journey of Tai-me.* Santa Barbara: University of California Press, 1967.

————. *The Way to Rainy Mountain.* Albuquerque: University of New Mexico Press, 1969.

Nabokov, Peter. *Two Leggings: The Making of a Crow Warrior.* New York: Thomas Y. Crowell, 1970.

Neihardt, John G. *Black Elk Speaks, Being the Life Story of a Holy Man of the Oglala Sioux.* Lincoln: University of Nebraska Press, 1961.

Peterson, Karen Daniels. *Howling Wolf, A Cheyenne Warrior's Graphic Interpretation of His People.* Palo Alto: American West Publishing Co., 1968.

————. *Plains Indian Art from Fort Marion.* Norman: University of Oklahoma Press, 1970.

Schultz, James Willard. *Apauk, Caller of Buffalo.* Boston: Houghton Mifflin, 1916.

Standing Bear, Chief Luther. *Land of the Spotted Eagle.* Boston: Houghton Mifflin, 1933.

————. *My Indian Boyhood.* Boston: Houghton Mifflin, 1931.

————. *My People the Sioux.* Boston: Houghton Mifflin, 1928.

Stirling, M. W. "Three Pictographic Autobiographies of Sitting Bull." *Smithsonian Miscellaneous Collections,* vol. 97, no. 5 (1938), 1-57.

Vestal, Stanley *Warpath, The True Story of the Fighting Sioux, Told in a Biography of Chief White Bull.* Boston: Houghton Mifflin, 1934.

Wallis, Wilson D. "Sun Dance of the Canadian Dakota." *Sun Dance of the Plains Indians.* Anthropological Papers of the American Museum of Natural History, 16 (1919), 317-81.

SECONDARY SOURCES

Bad Heart Bull, Amos. *A Pictographic History of the Oglala Sioux.* Text by Helen H. Blish. Lincoln: University of Nebraska Press, 1967.

Barbeau, Marius. *Indian Days on the Western Prairies.* Ottawa: National Museum of Canada, 1960.

Brown, Joseph Epes. *The Sacred Pipe, Black Elk's Account of the Seven Rites of the Oglala Sioux.* Norman: University of Oklahoma Press, 1967.

Dawdy, Doris Ostrander. *Annotated Bibliography of American Indian Painting.* New York: Museum of the American Indian, Heye Foundation, 1968.

Driver, Harold E. *Indians of North America.* Chicago: University of Chicago Press, 1969.

Ewers, John Canfield. *Plains Indian Painting, A Description of an Aboriginal American Art.* Palo Alto: Stanford University Press, 1939.

Gottschalk, Louis, Clyde Kluckhohn, and Robert Angell, eds. *The Use of Personal Documents in History, Anthropology, and Social Science.* Bulletin 53. New York: Social Science Research Council, 1945.

Hirschfelder, Arlene B. *American Indian Authors, A Representative Bibliography.* New York: Association on American Indian Affairs, 1970.

Kennedy, Michael Stephen. *The Assiniboines, From the Accounts of the Old Ones, Told to First Boy (James Larpenteur Long).* Norman: University of Oklahoma Press, 1961.

Langness, L. L. *The Life History in Anthropological Science.* New York: Holt, Rinehart and Winston, 1965.

Momaday, N. Scott. "The Man Made of Words." In *Indian Voices.* San Francisco: The Indian Historian Press, 1970.

Sayre, Robert F. "Vision and Experience in *Black Elk Speaks.*" *College English,* 32 (Feb. 1971), 509-35.

Stands in Timber, John. *Cheyenne Memories.* Lincoln: University of Nebraska Press, 1972.

Storm, Hyemeyohsts. *Seven Arrows.* New York: Harper and Row, 1972.

Vestal, Stanley. *New Sources of Indian History, 1850-1891.* Norman: University of Oklahoma Press, 1934.

———. *Sitting Bull, Champion of the Sioux, A Biography.* Boston: Houghton Mifflin, 1932.

Wildschut, William. "A Crow Pictographic Robe." *Indian Notes,* 3 (Jan. 1926), 28-32.